Hot Dog

Trevor Millum

D1798305

04897

Oxford University Press 1995

Hot Dog

1
A Trip to the Sun

I didn't really want to go on holiday with mum and dad. When you are 15 you want to be doing different things from your parents. They said I could bring a friend but who could I ask to spend 10 days with us? Me, mum, and dad and a hot beach? My mum looks so embarrassing in her swimsuit and dad's belly should have a Tetley's bitter logo on it. He struts along the beach like a peacock. Who does he think is looking at him?

Anyway, I agreed to go. It was better than staying at home with Aunt Doreen coming over to 'look after me'. She would make me go to bed at ten and ask questions about girl-friends. Girl-friends! A chance would be a fine thing. Ever since Wendy Worsley I had realized that fancying a girl and having a girl-friend were two very different things.

I'd sat next to Wendy on the school bus for a week and half and I thought we were getting on really well. I'd even done her Maths homework for her. Then she asked me not to sit next to her any more in case people started talking. Started talking! I took the hint. She ignores me now, even though I did her homework for her – twice. Perhaps it would have helped if the answers had been right.

So there I was on the plane to 'Paradise in the Sun'. I was wedged in between mum and dad. Mum was reading the in-flight magazine and checking that she knew where the emergency exits were. Dad was doing some 'easy listening' through his little red headphones.

I was trying to get a better look at the girl in the row in front on the other side of the gangway. She turned round a couple of times. She reminded me of Ripley, the heroine in *Aliens* – but younger, of course.

I squeezed past mum and walked slowly towards the toilets. I glanced down at the girl. She looked up at me briefly before returning to her book.

When I got into the toilet I looked at my face in the mirror. Not too bad. A bit pale – but some sun would soon fix that. Hair all right. I tried a grown-up, confident smile. It looked sickly and not very convincing.

Time to walk back and impress the girl with the black hair. How did these stupid doors open? I rattled and pushed. Then I realized I had to pull. The door jerked open and there she was. I had no time for a confident smile. No time for a few words she would remember. What could I say? 'Don't forget to wash your hands'? 'Please leave the basin clean'?

Then it was too late. The toilet door slammed shut and I was left to walk back past her empty seat.

I saw her a few times in the queues when we landed. I stood next to her as the luggage came round on the conveyor belt. Perhaps I could help with her bag. Perhaps I could start a conversation. – 'Hi! That's a lovely hold-all you have there! What pretty handles!' Perhaps I could spot a name tag on her luggage.

As I was day-dreaming, she reached for a bag. It had an address tag on it but the writing was too small to read. Then dad called me to help. Of course, we had more bags than anyone else. Mum had one bag full of shoes, Dad said. We piled them on the trolley and I pushed it. I pushed as fast as I could but the girl with black hair had got away.

2
Found and Lost

We were staying in a house which the travel company called a 'villa'. It was not much like the Roman villa we had sketched at school but it was okay. It even had an attractive little walled garden with a couple of lemon trees. I could not get over seeing real lemons growing on trees. An arched doorway led out from the yard to the side street.

Time passed slowly. I spent a lot of it playing patience on the coffee table or kicking a ball around the yard. There were no flowers to damage and no lawn to worry about. Dad spent a lot of time seeing if the local beers were all right and mum was busy getting the right amount of sun. 'Getting brown but not getting burnt,' she kept saying. 'It's an art.'

Once, when I was out, I saw the girl from the plane. She was looking at postcards in one of the shops on the other side of the market square. I suddenly felt the need to send a postcard to Aunt Doreen. By the time I reached the shop the girl had moved on. I spotted her looking at melons at a fruit stall a little way down the street. 'Some fruit would do me good,' I thought.

Then she was off again. She walked down a side street, carrying her shopping. Perhaps I could follow her and discover where she was staying. It must be quite close to our villa. I used the little shops and pavement traders for cover. 'This is easy,' I thought. 'I don't know why they make such a fuss about it in films.'

Someone clutched my arm. Surely not mum? No, it was a short, dark man with a very hairy chest and a striped shirt that was much too small. He smiled, 'Ah, young man. You have a nice girl-friend, yes?'

'How does he know?' I thought. He couldn't know. And anyway I hadn't got a girl-friend, had I? I was confused but it did not stop him going on.

'A nice bracelet for your girl-friend? Look at this! See the workmanship. I make you a special price, no?'

By the time I had convinced him that I had not got a girl-friend or any spare money, it was too late. She had disappeared. I walked further along the street but she had gone.

Although I had lost her I did not feel disappointed. I felt cheerful. At least she was nearby and I might bump into her at any time. Then I remembered Wendy Worsley. The girl from the plane might be just like her. I could imagine her saying, 'Stop following me about, people will start to talk.'

3
Ginger

On Wednesday, it happened. Mum was having a siesta in the bedroom. Dad had fallen asleep on the sun-lounger on the balcony. There was a knock at the front door. Who could it be? Someone selling something? I opened the big wooden door. There, standing in the sun, was the girl. She had a dog on a lead. It was like a dream.

She looked quite nervous. 'Hello,' she said. 'Er... I wonder if you can help me...'

I should have asked her in, I should have offered her a drink. I just stood there, grinning.

'We were on the same plane,' she said, 'and I noticed where you were staying. You see, it's the dog...'

I looked at the dog. An ordinary scruffy-looking animal – a sort of terrier, rather sorry for itself. And it was not on a proper lead, it was a piece of string.

She explained that they had found the dog in the yard of their house. 'It might just be a stray, but it seems too friendly.'

'Is it safe?' I asked.

'You mean has it got rabies? Well, mum says
it's all right – and she's an expert on that kind
of thing. But she's allergic to dogs. She can't
have them near her and she's in a right panic.
She'll just put it out on the street.'

I nearly said, 'Why worry. That's where it came from.' But I stopped myself. If she was a dog-lover, I could be a dog-lover too.

'What's its name?' I asked.

'Ginger,' she said, without a pause.

'And what's your name?' I asked. It felt like the most daring thing I'd ever done.

'Jenny.' Then she did pause. 'Can you look after him?' She smiled at me and fluttered her eye lashes. I really wanted to look after that dirty mongrel more than anything. It could

sleep in my bed if that would please her. I had to think of something that would make sense to mum and dad. But how? Where?

'Of course,' I said. 'We've got a yard, too – you know, a bit of garden with a wall round it. Come on.'

I closed the door quietly behind me. We walked down the path at the side and through the door under the archway. 'Look,' I said, as if I had built it myself, 'it's perfect.' And it was. A walled area about six by four metres with two gnarled lemon trees and an old creeper struggling up the side of the house. There was even a low shelter with the remains of firewood in it from last winter. 'That'll do for a kennel,' I said proudly.

She looked so pleased I thought she was going to kiss me. But no such luck. She just handed me the string and said, 'I'll come round each day and take him for a walk.'

'What about food?'

'We'll have to see what we can find. I don't know if we can buy dog food here.' I liked the way she said 'we'. I was happy for the rest of the day. If I had been a dog I would have run around the house, barking and jumping up and licking people's faces. I didn't. Luckily, Ginger didn't either.

Telling mum and dad about Ginger was quite easy in the end. I told them he was a stray I had found and that I was hoping for a big reward. I was going to put up 'Found' notices. It would be good translation practice. They were used to my mad plans. Maybe they thought it would give me something to do. Mum even brought back some cheap bits of meat when she went shopping.

4
Ants

Ginger seemed happy enough. He was a quiet good-tempered dog, glad to see anyone who gave him food or attention.

On Friday evening I stayed in. Mum and dad went down to the bar on the beach. I had not seen Jenny that day but Ginger had been fed so I think she had called while we were out. He was not as excited as usual when I brought him some leftovers. She might call again, I thought. I got out Dad's personal stereo and put on my favourite tape.

Frenzied barking interrupted the music. I ran to the back door and out into the yard. Ginger was in a dreadful state. He was scratching and shaking and howling and barking all at the same time. I could not understand what was the matter.

'What's up, Ginge? Something scare you?' I looked around. Everything seemed to be all right. Then I felt a sharp nip on my ankle, then another. I pulled up the leg of my jeans. Ants! Ants everywhere – and mainly on poor old Ginger.

Another nip, further up my leg.

'Hold on, Ginger, I'll be back.' I ran inside, tore off my jeans, socks, and trainers, T-shirt too – anything that might hide an ant. I grabbed the insect spray and sprayed my legs. 'New Bug Killer for Men! What a pong!' But if it kept the ants off me, I didn't care.

I hunted for something to wear on my feet. If only I had brought my wellingtons. Then I remembered mum's bag of shoes. I ran to her room. Wow, she really had brought them all. I found her big leather boots and squeezed into them. It was lucky that she had big feet.

Ginger was still barking madly when I hobbled back to the yard, ready to do battle with the ants to save Jenny's dog. I held him by the collar while I used the insect spray. It was not easy and Ginger would not stop barking.

Then the street door clicked. I looked up. It was Jenny. Oh no! She stared. There I was, dressed in underpants and mum's best leather boots, spraying the legs of her dog. What would she think?

She didn't run away, which was good. She didn't scream or giggle, which was even better.

'Look out, Jenny,' I said. 'There are millions of ants everywhere. I've got rid of most of them with this spray. Poor Ginger was covered in them.'

Jenny was great. She held Ginger while I gave him a final spray. She put a hand over his eyes and nose. 'I heard him barking,' she said. 'I knew it was him.'

I nodded.

'He needs a wash,' she said. 'He's covered all over in insect spray and dead ants.'

'No hose pipe here,' I replied. 'But there's a bucket.'

While Jenny tried to calm Ginger, I filled the big plastic bucket and carried it outside. 'Watch out!' I called and chucked the water over Ginger.

My aim was not good. Half of it went over Ginger and the other half went over Jenny. She let go of Ginger. He was furious. She was soaked and I felt stupid. Oh no, I thought, that's done it. But she laughed. An idiot in boots and underpants throws water all over her and she laughs. I felt so happy I almost hugged her. I am glad I didn't because just then mum and dad walked in.

They expected to see a dog in the yard. They didn't expect to see a wet dog in a state of shock. They certainly did not expect to see their son in his underpants giggling with a half-drowned young girl they had never met before.

It took a lot of talking to calm them down and a lot of patting and stroking to calm Ginger down. But in the end mum lent Jenny a dry T-shirt, I put some ant-free clothes on, and we all had coffee on the balcony. Things returned to normal – which was a shame in some ways.

5

A Dream Come True

Jenny came round each day from then on and sometimes we took Ginger for a walk together. She made him a new collar with the name tag from her travel bag. We walked the streets and sometimes stopped at a café for a drink. 'Hey!' I thought, 'I'm here with the girl of my dreams – and I didn't even have to ask her out.'

The sun shone. Time passed.

Then Ginger's owner turned up. Jenny

brought him round to see me and to collect the dog. 'This is Gino,' she said. I wished he was not so good-looking and I wished she had not called him Gino. Mister Gino or something like that would have been much better.

Gino's house was next to Jenny's villa. He had been away for a while, leaving the dog in the care of the housekeeper. She came in once a day. 'When I return home, the dog, he is gone. My housekeeper has not bothered to search. But I try next door. And your friend Jenny has told me of your great kindness.'

The dog's name was not Ginger, of course. It was something like Antonio Diego de Parador. The name was much too long for a dog like Ginger. It turned out he was an expensive pedigree! Jenny took off his collar and held it as if it was something precious.

Ginger was pleased to see Gino. He went off with his owner without another glance at me or Jenny. I bet he won't even send us a Christmas card. But Gino thanked us many times. He even gave us some money – but money didn't make up for losing Jenny. No Ginger, no Jenny, I realized. She watched Gino and Ginger disappear down the street.

Then she smiled and said, 'Oh, well, see you,' and off she went. She seemed sad but I thought it had more to do with saying goodbye to Ginger than to me.

'See you,' I replied.

But I didn't see her again. She didn't call round. If I had been a dog she might have called. I thought of running through the streets on all fours and howling outside her window.

Perhaps she needed an excuse to visit me. Perhaps the memory of me standing in underpants and women's boots was too much for her. Of course, I should have found out where she lived. But I hadn't and now I regretted it. The last few days of the holiday were quiet and I spent a lot of time thinking.

6
Up in the Air

I did see Jenny at the airport but she didn't see me. If I did bump into her again, what would I say? 'Found any good dogs lately?' or 'Fancy a poodle or a labrador next?'

As soon as we were up in the air, mum fell asleep. Dad put on his earphones and got lost in his easy listening. I walked down the gangway towards the toilets. While I waited for one to become free, I looked back up the plane. No Jenny in sight.

A handle turned. The door slid open. Jenny stood in front of me. 'Ah,' she said, 'there you are.' She smiled and put something in my hand. 'Thanks. See you.' She walked back down the plane. I stood with my mouth open.

I stepped inside the little cubicle, shut the door and looked at what was in my hand. Ginger's collar. A nice thought – but why bother? The address tag was still attached. I looked at it more closely. It didn't say Ginger. It said Jennifer Flynn and was followed by an address and a telephone number.

I smiled confidently into the mirror and decided that the first thing I must do when we got home was get a dog.

JENNIFER FLYNN
126 HIGH ST.
ASHTON, SURREY
TEL: 01634 2005

❖ ❖ ❖

Oxford University Press, Walton Street, Oxford, OX2 6DP

Oxford New York
Athens Auckland Bangkok Bombay
Calcutta Cape Town Dar es Salaam Delhi
Florence Hong Kong Istanbul Karachi
Kuala Lumpur Madras Madrid Melbourne
Mexico City Nairobi Paris Singapore
Taipei Tokyo Toronto

and associated companies in
Berlin Ibadan

Oxford is a trade mark of Oxford University Press

Printed in Great Britain

Illustrations by Adam Stower